Secrets of the Dolphins

By K. C. Kelley

The Child's World®
www.childsworld.com

Published in the United States of America by The Child's World®
P.O. Box 326 • Chanhassen, MN 55317-0326
800-599-READ • www.childsworld.com

ACKNOWLEDGMENTS

The Child's World®: Mary Berendes, Publishing Director

Produced by Shoreline Publishing Group LLC
President / Editorial Director: James Buckley, Jr.
Designer: Tom Carling, carlingdesign.com
Cover Art: Slimfilms
Copy Editor: Beth Adelman

Photo Credits
Cover—Photos.com (3)
Interior—AP/Wide World: 20, 25, 26, 27; Corbis: 10, 16, 17;
Dreamstime.com: 5, 8, 13; iStock: 9, 23, 24; Minden Pictures: 6, 7, 14,
20, 18, 21, 28

Copyright © 2007 by The Child's World®
All rights reserved. No part of this book may be reproduced or
utilized in any form or by any means without written permission
from the publisher.

LIBRARY OF CONGRESS CATALOGING-IN-PUBLICATION DATA

Kelley, K. C.
  Secrets of the dolphins / by K.C. Kelley.
     p. cm. — (Girls rock!)
  Includes bibliographical references and index.
  ISBN 1-59296-747-7 (library bound : alk. paper)
  1. Dolphins—Juvenile literature. I. Title. II. Series.
  QL737.C432K44 2006
  599.53—dc22

                              2006004606

CONTENTS

ALL ABOUT Me!

Hi! This book is all about me and my family. Who am I? Well, I'd tell you my name, but it's too hard to spell in your language! Let's just say that I'm a dolphin, and I'm here to fill you in on a dolphin's life.

Dolphins like me aren't fish. We're actually **mammals**, like dogs and elephants and, well . . . like you!

We're **marine** mammals, which means we live in the ocean all the time. Unlike fish, though, we have to breathe air at the surface of the water. That's why people often see us popping our heads out of the water.

Here's what I look like. I'm a bottlenose dolphin.

There are about 40 types of dolphins. The bottlenose dolphin is the most common.

Say hello to a porpoise!

Many people confuse dolphins with porpoises. Porpoises are another kind of marine mammal. Here's how you can tell the difference between us: The picture on the opposite page shows my pals, the **dusky** dolphins. The picture below is a porpoise. See how our dolphin noses are more pointed, while the porpoise's nose is more rounded?

Our teeth are different, too. Look at my choppers on page 5. Notice how each one is pointed and sharp?

If you could look inside a porpoise's mouth (watch your fingers!), you'd see that its teeth are shaped more like small spades.

Most of us dolphins are gray. These dusky dolphins are gray and black.

Fish or Dolphin?

To make things even more confusing, people sometimes use the name "dolphin" for a kind of fish! This fish is also known as a dorado or mahi-mahi.

Here I am, coming to the surface to breathe. You can see the blowhole on the top of my head. The blowhole closes when I go back underwater.

As I said, I have to come to the surface to breathe. I take in air through a **blowhole** on the top of my head. This makes it hard to wear a hat (ha, ha . . . that's an old dolphin joke). Our blowholes make us easy to spot if you're looking for us.

I weigh about 400 pounds (181 kg) and I'm about 8 feet (2 m) long. That's about average for a bottlenose dolphin.

My skin is smooth and slippery and helps me slice through the water easily. I have a flipper on each side of my body. On my back is a **dorsal** fin. Like human faces or fingerprints, dorsal fins are different on every dolphin.

We're not being rude, we're just giving you a good look at our tail flukes.

My tail has two wide parts called **flukes**. I wave them up and down to speed through the water in search of fish . . . or fun!

The rounded part on the top of my head helps me hear sounds in the water.

Have you ever heard an echo? That's when you make a sound and it bounces back to you, a little quieter. We dolphins use something like that to find our way around. We use

echolocation. That means we send out noises and listen for them to bounce back. We use the echoes from our sounds to "see" what's out in front of us.

At the top of my head is a "melon" . . . no, not the fruit! My melon is a part of my body that helps me "read" the sounds that bounce back.

We also use echolocation to help us find food. The sounds we send out bounce back to us when they hit tasty fish! Time to eat!

Other animals use echolocation to find food and find their way around. Bats use echolocation to help them "see" when they fly at night.

We dolphins can also whistle—although to humans, it might sound like a squeak. We use this sort of sound to communicate between ourselves. It helps us find our families and tell each other about food or danger.

Some scientists think we also communicate by jumping, tail-walking (as we're doing here), or using our **flippers**. Since the scientists never asked me about this, they're still not completely sure!

Now that you know more about us and how we get around and communicate, let's take a tour of my watery home.

Are we doing this to communicate or just to have fun? We're not telling!

WHERE I Live

I live in the ocean. Our cousins, the whales, live in the ocean, too. Actually, dolphins, porpoises, and whales are all part of the same family. We're called **cetaceans** (seh-TAY-shenz).

Cetaceans often swim along near the surface of the ocean. After we get a breath, we can dive down to look for food. Whales can dive much deeper than we can—they're much bigger, after all. Most of us dolphins don't dive much more that 150 feet (46 m).

OPPOSITE PAGE
Here are some dolphins I know popping up to get a breath of air. If you want to see dolphins in the ocean, look for those fins poking up above the surface of the water.

This Amazon River dolphin has a long, pointy snout. It's perfect for finding food among the rocks on the river bottom.

Here's something cool— not all dolphins live in the ocean. Several kinds live in large rivers instead. The Amazon River dolphin, which is also called a *boutu* (BOO-too), lives in the Amazon River in South America. The Irrawaddy and Ganges River dolphins live in rivers in Asia and India.

Ganges dolphins have terrible eyesight, but they have long, pointy noses to help them search for food. The rarest type of dolphin, the *baiji* (bai-EE-jee), lives in in China. It is well known for its light pink color.

A species is a particular type of an animal. A threatened species is one that is in some danger of dying out.

Sadly, most river dolphins are **threatened species**.

Like all other river dolphins, the Irrawaddy dolphin lives in freshwater, not salty ocean water. Its nose isn't pointy, but trust me, it's a dolphin!

Watch out, fish, here I come! Here I'm chasing a school of snacks . . . I mean fish!

So, let's go back to the ocean. What do I like to eat out here? I especially like mackerel, a type of small fish. Herring is good, too, and so is squid! I also like shrimp and sardines.

Sometimes I also eat shellfish such as clams or mussels.

I work with other dolphins to find food. One trick we use is to circle around a group of fish. It's like a cowboy corralling some steers! We also go under a school of fish and blow bubbles. The bubbles make the fish rise to the surface, where they're easier to catch.

Like other mammals, we have live babies instead of laying eggs. Our babies pop out ready to swim and eat. Here's something cool— dolphins are the only mammals that are naturally born tail first!

Surf's Up!

You think you humans are the only ones who can surf? Check this out! When we see a good wave, we can surf *inside* it!

My mom took good care of me. She stuck with me for about three years—that's a long time in the animal world. When I was a baby, I weighed about 40 pounds (18 kg) and was about 4 feet (1 m) long. We lived in a **pod**, which is a group of dolphins. In a pod, all the moms help each other.

Dolphins like to live together. It's unusual to see one dolphin alone. Usually, we're in pods like this one.

PEOPLE AND Me

3

Dolphins are very friendly, and we spend lots of time near the surface. We're pretty curious, too. When we see boats out on the ocean, we often swim by to take a look. That's why dolphins and people have known about each other since people first started sailing.

Even if you've never seen us out at sea, you might have seen us in **aquarium**

"Very nice to meet you!" At dolphin shows, you might get a chance to shake my hand, or should I say, my flipper!

shows. We work with human trainers to learn things that will entertain visitors. Some shows let humans swim with dolphins. Our shows help people learn more about us. And the more that people know about us, the more it helps our brothers and sisters in the ocean.

Handy Tools

Or should we say "nosy tools"? Some of my dolphin cousins near Australia have learned to use sponges to help find food. These sponges are undersea creatures that are soft and squishy. Some of my cousins pull up sponges and put them on their noses when they poke around in sharp coral. That way, they don't get hurt! The amazing thing is that the mother dolphins teach their young to do this!

Along with entertaining people, we also help them. Along some seacoasts, we help people fish. We chase the fish toward shore, where people wait with nets. We keep some of the fish in return!

The U.S. Navy has trained us to help find underwater **mines** or other explosives. We dive down, spot the mines, and come back up to let the human divers take over the dangerous part.

We can live outside of the water for a short time. This dolphin helping the U.S. Navy in the Red Sea got a ride in a boat!

People tell lots of stories about dolphins helping shipwrecked sailors. Some divers talk about dolphins helping them when they were having trouble.

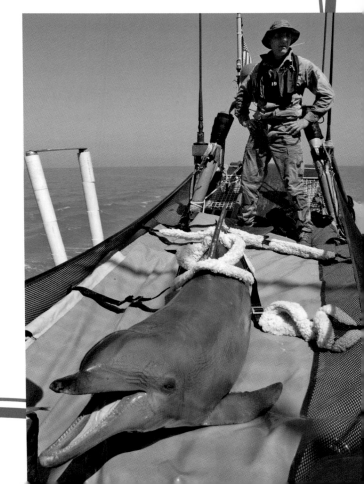

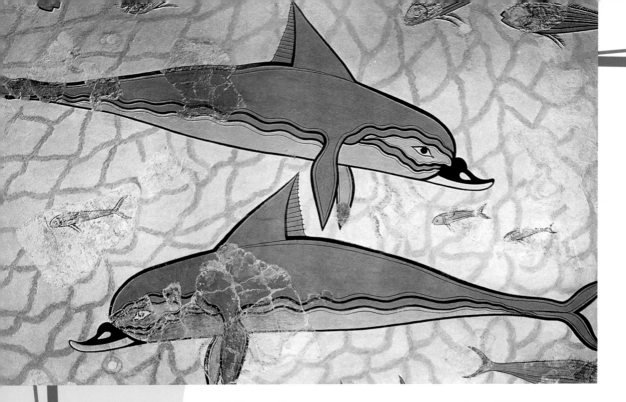

This colorful painting of dolphins was found in ancient ruins on an island near Greece.

You humans seem to like us a lot. You've included us in your artwork for many years. There are paintings of dolphins on ancient Greek temples. Artists have painted pictures of us. Sculptors have carved us in marble. The British Virgin Islands put us on a coin.

People have made movies and TV shows about us! The best known were about a dolphin named Flipper, who had lots of adventures with his human friends. In the first TV series, Flipper was played by a dolphin named Mitzi, who was a good actor!

Here's Mitzi showing off for Brian Kelly, her costar on the first Flipper TV show. The show ran from 1964 to 1968.

One more thing before I splash on out of here. People and dolphins have gotten along for hundreds of years. But some of the things people do hurt us. Sometimes we get caught in fishing nets. And pollution and garbage in the water harm us and the foods we eat.

The good news is that many people are working to help keep us safe. Some fishing boats now use nets that we can get out of more easily. And some people are working to reduce the

Want to help? Some groups working with dolphins let you "adopt" one of us. While you learn more about dolphins, you'll help keep us safe!

amount of pollution that gets into our oceans. I hope you've learned more about us. Next time you see a dolphin, make sure to say hi—it just might be me!

After they helped this sick dolphin recover, scientists took it back to its ocean home.

GLOSSARY

aquarium a place or a tank where people can look at animals that live in the water

blowhole the hole on top of the head that a dolphin or whale uses for breathing

cetaceans the scientific name of the family of creatures that includes dolphins and whales

dorsal something that's on the back, like a dorsal fin

dusky somewhat dark or shadowy

echolocation the ability to use sounds and their echoes to find your way or find food

flippers the fins on the sides of a dolphin's body

flukes the wider parts at the end of a sea creature's tail

mammals warm-blooded animals that give birth to babies (not eggs) and feed their babies milk from their bodies

marine having to do with the ocean

mines bombs placed in the water

pod a group of dolphins that live together

threatened species a type of animal that has low numbers and has a chance of dying out altogether

FIND OUT MORE

BOOKS

Dolphins
by Sylvia James
(Mondo Publishing, New York) 2001
This book includes pictures and charts that help you learn more about dolphins.

Dolphins & Porpoises
by Beth Wagner Brust
(Wildlife Education/ZooBooks, Poway, CA) 2003
A colorful book that brings these animals to life, from their habits to their work with humans.

Eyewitness Whales, Dolphins, and Porpoises
by Mark Carwardine
(DK Publishing, New York) 1995
This lively book about marine mammals includes lots of pictures, including close-ups and cutaways.

WEB SITES

Visit our home page for lots of links about dolphins, porpoises, and other marine mammals: www.childsworld.com/links

Note to Parents, Teachers, and Librarians: We routinely check our Web links to make sure they're safe, active sites—so encourage your readers to check them out!

INDEX

K. C. Kelley isn't really a dolphin—he just imagined that he was to write this book. He has written dozens of nonfiction books for young readers, on everything from NASCAR to baseball to dinosaurs. He lives in Santa Barbara, California, and can see dolphins playing in the ocean from the beach near his house.